Movements in Art **THE RENAISSANCE**

Movements in Art THE RENAISSANCE

ANNE FITZPATRICK

CREATIVE EDUCATION

Published by Creative Education
123 South Broad Street, Mankato, Minnesota 56001
Creative Education is an imprint of The Creative Company

Design and production by Blue Design (www.bluedes.com)
Art direction by Rita Marshall

Photographs by Corbis (Alinari Archives, Archivo Iconografico, S.A., Arte &
Immagini srl, Bettmann, Burstein Collection, Elio Ciol, Stephanie Colasanti,
Edimédia, Historical Picture Archive, David Lees, National Gallery Collection;
By kind permission of the Trustees of the National Gallery, London, Gianni
Dagli Orti, Huber Stadler, Summerfield Press, Sandro Vannini, Michael S.
Yamashita), Getty Images (Albrecht Dürer)

Library of Congress Cataloging-in-Publication Data

Fitzpatrick, Anne, 1978–
The Renaissance / by Anne Fitzpatrick.
p. cm. — (Movements in art)
Includes index.
ISBN 1-58341-349-9
1. Art, Renaissance—Juvenile literature. I. Title. II. Series.

N6370.F57 2004
709'.02'4—dc22   2004055270

First edition

9 8 7 6 5 4 3 2 1

Cover: Self-portrait of Albrecht Dürer (c. 1500)
Page 2: Study for a mural by Leonardo da Vinci (c. 1503–06)
Pages 4–5: Uffizi Gallery

The Renaissance

The history of the world can be told through accounts of great battles, the lives of kings and queens, and the discoveries and inventions of scientists and explorers. But the history of the way people think and feel about themselves and the world is told through art. From paintings of the hunt in prehistoric caves, to sacred art in the European Middle Ages, to the abstract forms of the 20th century, movements in art are the expression of a culture. Sometimes that expression is so powerful and compelling that it reaches through time to carry its message to another generation.

Lasting from the 14th to the mid-17th century, the Renaissance produced such masterpieces as the dome of St. Peter's Basilica (opposite), designed by Michelangelo, and *Saint Sebastian* (c. 1490, above), by Pietro Perugino.

THE PLAGUE

In 1348, Italian ships arrived from China at an English seaport with several crew members dying from a mysterious illness. Within days, the disease spread throughout the city. Within a year, it had spread across Europe. The "Black Death," as it was known, appeared first as a fever. Then red spots appeared on the skin and began to turn black. It was extremely infectious and was often carried by fleas on rats. Because agriculture and trade suffered as people tried to

stop the spread of disease, plague was often followed by famine. The worst attacks were over by 1390, by which time about one-third of the population of Europe had died. Small outbreaks continued to occur until the 17th century.

In two of the world's largest art museums, the crowds pass paintings and sculptures in room after room with hardly a glance. In the Louvre Museum of Paris, they finally stop in front of a tiny painting covered in bulletproof glass: the *Mona Lisa*. In the Vatican Museums of Rome, the crowds pour through a narrow door into an empty room and look up at the ceiling of the Sistine Chapel. Michelangelo painted it just five years after Leonardo da Vinci painted the *Mona Lisa*, during the period of history known as the Renaissance. The way people of the Renaissance thought and felt about themselves and the world was expressed in some of the greatest art in history, and it still resonates with us today.

THE REBIRTH

Western Europe was changing as the 15th century dawned. The population was greatly decreased by the plagues and famines of the previous century, and this gave the people who worked the land more power over their wealthy landlords. They demanded hourly wages or bought their own land as great estates were broken up. Towns and cities were growing larger as trade increased and dependence on agriculture declined. Communities of specialized **craftsmen** formed and prospered in the new

As towns and cities began to flourish across Europe during the Renaissance, many people opened their own shops, with living quarters above them, in cobblestoned market squares (left). Larger cities and towns, such as Constantinople (below), were often fortified with massive walls.

The bronze *Miracle of the Ass* (1447–50), in which the figures appear to float in front of the background, is one of 29 pieces of sculpture that Donatello created for the Basilica di Sant'Antonio's *High Altar of St. Anthony*.

urban centers. Instead of feeling restricted by the family or occupation into which they were born, people began to think of themselves as individuals, with God-given power to shape and control their destiny and environment. At the same time, improved sailing technology allowed Europeans to sail farther and farther away. They learned more about the lands beyond their own shores and began to think of Europe as the center of the Christian world.

Many people were conscious of the change in the air and recognized that there was something new and wonderful happening. In Italy, it was thought of as a rebirth of the ideas and energy of ancient Rome. During the **Middle Ages**, the technological, **philosophical**, and artistic accomplishments of **Classical** Greece and Rome had been dismissed as the unholy acts of pagan civilizations. But Renaissance thinkers sought to break away from medieval ideas, and they saw continuity between Roman antiquity and "modern" times. This was not a return to the past, or to paganism. They were building upon the achievements of the Classical period to achieve a new era of greatness in the name of Christianity. The Classical ideals of reason, moderation, and proportion now expressed the dignity of a humanity created by God and given free will and dominion over the world.

Florence, in northern Italy, was the largest city in Europe in the 15th century. It was an independent republic governed by wealthy merchants and **guilds**. In an atmosphere of prosperity and freedom, the artistic and intellectual community of Florence flourished. Two of its giants, the architect and painter Filippo Brunelleschi (1377–1446) and the sculptor Donatello (Donato di Niccolo di Betto Bardi, c. 1386–1466), went to Rome to study ancient ruins. Brunelleschi reintroduced features of Classical architecture, such as

The marble *David* (1409) is the earliest work attributed to Donatello and reflects his careful study of marble works from antiquity. Unlike his later bronze *David*, this sculpture shows David clothed and standing in a traditional posture of victory above the head of the slain Goliath.

Brothers Hubert and Jan van Eyck, artists from northern Europe, created the *Ghent Altarpiece*, a brilliantly colored painting that depicts angels, the Virgin Mary, Christ, St. John the Baptist, and, below them, heaven in careful detail.

columned arcades and emphasis on creating **harmonious** proportions, in the buildings he designed in Florence. Donatello began carving large-scale, freestanding statues instead of the **relief** sculptures that had been prevalent since the end of the Roman Empire in the fifth century. His figures were realistic and lifelike, in the Classical style.

Brunelleschi, Donatello, and other artists of Florence had constant discussions with each other about the depiction of **perspective**, space, and volume. They also talked to scholars and intellectuals about the science and mathematics of perspective and about their studies in Classical antiquity. Art was coming to be recognized as an intellectual pursuit. Artists were seen as more than just craftsmen as people realized that art required creativity and thought as well as skill and hard work.

A young **apprentice** in the workshop of the painter Masolino di Panicale (1383–1447) listened to these intellectual discussions and was influenced by them. Tommaso Guido (1401–28) was nicknamed "Masaccio," meaning "clumsy Tom," because he was so obsessed with art that he neglected everything else. Working on a series of **frescoes** in the Brancacci Chapel in Florence, he combined Brunelleschi's use of perspective with Donatello's naturalistic forms and the realistic light and color of his master Masolino to paint figures that had a real, physical presence. When he was just 27, Masaccio died so suddenly that many people

With realistic details and a perfect use of perspective, Masaccio's *The Tribute Money* (1426–27) depicts three moments in the story of the tax collector from the Bible's gospel of Matthew; the center shows part one, the left part two, and the right part three.

Although Perugino was not considered a religious artist, his *Virgin and Child with Two Saints* is one of many of his paintings to feature the religious subject matter so prominent in Renaissance art.

suspect he was poisoned. Although his career was cut short, Masaccio's innovations were a key turning point in the emergence of a new style. The Renaissance had begun.

Florence and northern Italy were the heart of the Renaissance movement, but important changes were occurring elsewhere, particularly in northern Europe. In Flanders (modern-day Belgium and northern France), painters were mixing their paints with oil instead of egg, which most artists of the time used. Oil paints could be applied in thinner, more fluid layers that gave the paintings a luminous quality. The fluid layers were easier to work with and dried more slowly, allowing the artist to work on a painting longer and create more subtle changes in color. The painters of Flanders made extremely realistic, detailed paintings with the new medium. They tried to keep the secret of oil painting to themselves, but eventually it spread to the rest of Europe. One story says that a young Italian apprentice in Flanders took the secret to Italy when his master died, barely escaping a professional killer hired by the outraged artists.

The art of northern Europe was also affected by religious turmoil leading up to the Protestant Reformation in 1517. New ideas about religion emphasized seeking a personal relationship with God. Artists assimilated this idea by portraying scenes from the Bible in contemporary settings. The scenes were painted realistically, with mundane details of everyday life in 15th-century Europe. The effect was to make Biblical stories seem familiar and accessible. Careful attention to detail and emphasis on faithful representation in **secular** paintings such as **portraits** and landscapes also reflected religious thought. The artists demonstrated their awareness of God

PLACE TO VISIT: THE UFFIZI GALLERY

The Uffizi Gallery in Florence boasts an extensive art collection begun by the Medici family. It is housed in a palace commissioned by Cosimo de' Medici in 1560. Visitors can spend days wandering through 45 rooms filled with one masterpiece after another. The collection includes works by Masolino and Masaccio, Fra Angelico,

Dürer, Verrocchio, Perugino, Botticelli (including *The Birth of Venus*), Leonardo, Raphael, Michelangelo, Titian, and Tintoretto. The city of Florence is filled with other Renaissance treasures, including the Palazzo Vecchio, another Medici palace; the great dome of the Santa Maria del Fiore Cathedral, designed by Brunelleschi; the Convent of San Marco, featuring Fra Angelico's *Annunciation*; Masaccio's frescoes in the Brancacci Chapel; and Michelangelo's *David* at the Gallery of the Academy. (Pictured: *Dead Christ* by Perugino)

in nature and daily life by recreating His world with worshipful attention to the smallest detail. Ordinary objects were often endowed with religious symbolism; for example, a chair in the corner of a painting might be decorated with a Biblical scene.

The religious turmoil in northern Europe affected Italian artists as well. The **pope** in Rome turned to artists to help strengthen his hold on the Catholic Church. The pope wanted to glorify Rome as the "capital of Christianity" by building new churches and palaces and filling them with sculptures and frescoes. The Roman Catholic Church also tried to incorporate the new emphasis on a personal relationship with God by reviving strict religious rules for everyday life and stressing **meditation** and reflection. Frescoes commissioned by the Church for churches and monasteries became more accessible and meditative.

The efforts of the Catholic Church also helped, unintentionally, to create a unified Renaissance style by increasing communication among artists across Europe. A series of international meetings was held in Switzerland, Germany, and Italy throughout the 15th century, at which the concerns of the Church were discussed; these meetings facilitated the exchange of ideas across Europe. They also ensured that many of the same issues, such as the nature of the **Eucharist**, were being discussed across Europe. The result was that similar **themes**, such as the Last Supper of Christ, began appearing in art in different parts of Europe.

Pope Leo X was dedicated to promoting the arts and commissioned many Renaissance artists, most notably Raphael, to complete important works in Rome.

Albrecht Dürer's love of nature and his devotion to depicting it accurately are evident in *The Vision of Saint Eustace* (1500), in which the saint kneels before a stag bearing a crucifix between his antlers.

ARTISTS OF THE RENAISSANCE

The leading artist of the German Renaissance, Albrecht Dürer (1471–1528), depicted the Last Supper in his series of **wood engravings** known as *The Passion* (1506–13). Wood engraving was new to Europe, made popular by Johann Gutenburg in Germany in 1452 as a method of printing books. Dürer's godfather was the first German book publisher, and Dürer learned wood engraving in his workshop in Nuremberg. He also learned a trade from his father, who was a goldsmith. But Dürer's ambition was to be an artist, and to raise the status of artists beyond that of craftsmen. When he was 15, he was apprenticed to an important local painter. At 19, he left Nuremberg and traveled to Italy, where he absorbed the ideas of the Italian Renaissance.

Dürer was impressed by the social standing of artists in Italy, observing that there, "I am a gentleman; at home I am a parasite." When he returned home, he sought the company of scholars and began to study geometry and mathematics. He painted a self-portrait in 1498 in which he was dressed in the elegant clothes of a gentleman, and another in 1500 in which he appeared as Christ to celebrate his God-given powers of creativity. In addition to his religious subjects and portraits, Dürer painted studies of animals and nature, recording what he saw to the tiniest detail.

Dürer's attention to detail may have been due to the influence of artists from Flanders, such as Jan van Eyck (1390–1441). He is known to have

Like many of his drawings, Leonardo da Vinci's *Head of a Woman* (c. 1500) reflects his careful study of the human form, as the viewer can almost see the delicate bone structure of the woman's graceful face.

seen van Eyck's *Ghent Altarpiece* (1432) and called it "stupendous." The **altarpiece** is a folding screen that is 11.5 feet (3.5 m) tall and 15 feet (4.6 m) wide. Despite its great size, the scenes depicted are painted with a minutely detailed style. The combination, as Dürer noted, is stunning. The piece was begun by Jan's brother Hubert van Eyck (1370–1426). When Hubert died in 1426, Jan finished the project. Jan achieved early success when his **patron**, the Duke of Burgundy, sent him to Portugal to paint Princess Isabella. The Duke was engaged to Isabella, but he had never met her. Jan sent back two portraits—one by land and one by sea—in case one got lost. The Duke must have liked them, because he married Isabella a short time later.

One of the great masters of the Italian Renaissance was Leonardo da Vinci (1452–1519). Leonardo was born near Florence. His parents were not married to each other, which during the Renaissance meant that he was not quite accepted socially. Alhough he was well-known in Florence for his extraordinary talent, the city's great patrons of art, the wealthy Medici family, ignored him. He spent most of his life working for foreign nobles, including Duke Ludovico Sforza of Milan and the French monarchy. But in spite of his stigma, young Leonardo was apprenticed to an important Florentine sculptor and painter named Andrea del Verrocchio (1435–88). He became friendly with two fellow apprentices who would also become celebrated artists: Sandro Botticelli (1445–1510) and Pietro Perugino (c. 1450–1523).

Leonardo was a painter, architect, sculptor, scientist, and scholar. None of his sculptures, buildings, or inventions survives today, but he left notebooks full of important discoveries and innovations. He was obsessed with flying machines, and he also drew the world's first cars, bicycles, machine guns,

THE MEDICIS

The Medici family built its wealth on banking and cloth manufacturing. They referred to themselves as *popolani*, of the people, even as their fortunes rose. The family included four popes and a queen of France, in addition to the powerful leaders of Florence. In 1434, Cosimo de' Medici gained control of the city

with the help of the people. He and his descendants remained in power for 60 years, throughout the height of the Florentine Renaissance. They are best-known today for their passionate patronage of art and architecture. Lorenzo de' Medici estimated in 1470 that his family had spent 663,755 gold florins (equivalent to more than $100 million today) on artistic and architectural commissions since 1435. (Pictured: Cosimo de' Medici)

PLACE TO VISIT: THE VATICAN MUSEUMS

The Sistine Chapel is in the Vatican Palace in Rome, today part of the massive Vatican Museums. In addition to Michelangelo's incomparable ceiling and *The Last Judgment*, which dominates the Chapel from behind the altar, the remaining walls of the Sistine Chapel are covered with frescoes by other famous Renaissance artists. The *Stanza della Segnatura* and two other rooms painted by Raphael can also be seen at the Palace. The Vatican Museums contain works by Fra Angelico, Leonardo, and Titian, as well as the collection of Classical sculptures that Michelangelo and other Renaissance artists studied. St. Peter's Basilica is next door, where one can see Michelangelo's *Pieta* and climb to the top of the dome he designed.

and tanks. In addition to engineering and aeronautics, Leonardo studied **anatomy**. He dissected the corpses of people who had been executed for crimes or who had died in hospitals for the homeless. Leonardo applied his knowledge of anatomy to give the people in his paintings realistic form. With his scientist's eye, he also observed that objects in the distance appear less detailed. He blended colors to create the smoky effect of distance in the backgrounds of his paintings.

Raphael Sanzio (1483–1520) was apprenticed to Leonardo's friend Perugino. He was born in the city of Urbino in northern Italy, where his father was a painter in the court of the duke. When he was just 25, Raphael went to Rome to paint frescoes on the walls of the pope's Vatican Palace. At the same time, Michelangelo Buonarroti (1475–1564) was working on the ceiling of the palace's Sistine Chapel. Although Michelangelo kept the Chapel locked, it is rumored that Raphael managed to sneak in and see it before it was finished. The influence of that stolen glimpse is apparent in the weight and build of Raphael's figures, which suggest Michelangelo's sculptured forms. Raphael incorporated many influences to create a unified Renaissance style. The harmony of organization, sense of drama, attention to detail, and depiction of space, perspective, and volume in Raphael's paintings make him the quintessential Renaissance painter.

Like Raphael, Michelangelo established his reputation early. He was born near Florence to a minor noble but was raised for a short time by a stonecutter's family when his mother was too ill to take care of him. He sometimes attributed his love of sculpture to his childhood with the stonecutters. Although he was apprenticed to a painter, Michelangelo loved the

Raphael's *The School of Athens* (1509) is a depiction of philosophy that includes figures representing astronomy, geometry, and arithmetic, at the center of which are the ancient philosophers Plato (with a white beard) and Aristotle.

sculptures of ancient Rome and the work of Donatello. He quickly became an accomplished sculptor himself, completing two of his greatest works, the *Pieta* (1497) and *David* (1501–04), before he turned 30.

Michelangelo was fiercely proud and often outspokenly critical of his fellow artists. He had a broken nose from a fistfight with a rival sculptor, and he once painted a critic into a picture, being smothered by a snake. He never took on any apprentices. It is even said that after beginning work on the Sistine Chapel with assistants, he fired them all, removed what had already been painted, and started over alone. Despite his melancholy nature and bad temper, Michelangelo's dedication and diligence were extraordinary. He often worked late into the night by the light of a candle attached to his head. In order to paint the ceiling of the Sistine Chapel, he spent more than 4 years 60 feet (18 m) in the air, with his head bent back and paint splattering his face. When he was done, he had painted more than 300 individual figures over more than 5,000 square feet (465 sq m). But in spite of the acclaim he received for the ceiling of the Chapel and the enormous fresco covering one wall, *The Last Judgment* (1536–41), Michelangelo resented the time they took away from sculpting.

Tiziano Vecellio, better known as Titian (c. 1486–1576), was Michelangelo's contemporary, but he lived most of his life in Venice. He seldom traveled, although many of his patrons were monarchs and wealthy nobles through-out Italy and Europe. Titian received many **commissions**, especially for portraits and depictions of scenes from Classical myths. He was considered the greatest portrait painter of his time. Charles V, the king of Spain, was so

Titian called *The Rape of Europa* (1559–62), part of a series of seven mythological subjects he created for King Philip II of Spain, poetry. Such imaginative visions of distant worlds led his contemporaries to regard Titian as an artistic genius.

pleased with Titian's portrait of him that he made the artist a count. Titian made a rare trip in 1545 to paint a portrait of the pope in Rome, where he encountered the exciting innovations being made by Michelangelo and other artists. He absorbed what he saw without losing his own very unique style. Titian was a master of rich, blazing color. In paintings such as *Diana and Callisto* (1559), he arranged the figures to create dynamic contrasts with the color of their skin and clothes. Their poses were dramatic and expressive, often frozen in mid-action. Like much of Renaissance art, it is easy to believe that at any moment Titian's paintings will come to life.

GREAT WORKS OF THE RENAISSANCE

The Arnolfini Marriage (1434) is painted with such perfection of living detail that it is not lifelike at all. It is an exquisite jewel of a painting that displays Jan van Eyck's mastery of the new oil paints. It was commissioned by a wealthy Italian banker, who is depicted with his wife at their house in Flanders. Light from a window on the left-hand side of the painting touches the couple and the objects in the room, giving them a gentle vibrancy. The artist's tiny brushstrokes are

The influence of both the elegant decorative style of past generations and the realistic style of the Renaissance can be seen in Fra Angelico's *The Annunciation*. Bright colors and devout facial expressions heighten the scene's emotion.

barely visible, so that the painting seems like a photograph. But no photograph could be this focused; even the tiny scenes from the life of Christ that decorate a mirror on the back wall can be identified. Ordinary objects litter the room, each with significance. Oranges, rare and exotic in Renaissance Europe, emphasize the couple's wealth. A single lit candle symbolizes the presence of God. Other religious references, such as a string of rosary beads, signify the couple's piety.

In a peaceful monastery in Florence, a friar known as Fra Angelico ("Angelic Brother") made paintings about piety his specialty. Fra Giovanni di Fiesole (1387–1455) approached painting as an act of devotion. His frescoes on the walls of the monastery of San Marco use carefully orchestrated geometry and proportion to create serenity and harmony as a guide for the monks' meditations and prayer. In a fresco on the wall of one monk's cell, the angel Gabriel tells the Virgin Mary that she will give birth to the son of God. The arches that frame the two figures are drawn with an adept grasp of perspective. The forms retreat into the painting, creating an illusion of space that invites the viewer to step inside and contemplate the moment of revelation. The *Annunciation* (1438–46) was not seen by anyone but the monks of San Marco until long after the Renaissance, but today it is considered one of the great works of the period.

Boticelli's *The Birth of Venus* was the first large-scale Renaissance painting with an exclusively secular subject. The painting depicts Venus, the goddess of love in Classical mythology, rising from the sea on a clamshell. According to the myth, Venus sprang full-grown from the foam of the sea. Botticelli copied the modest pose of an ancient Roman statue of Venus for his painting. The

A TIME OF WAR

Italy was divided among several city-states during the Renaissance. The largest were Venice, Milan, Florence, Naples, and the papal states, controlled by the pope in Rome. A tense balance of power was maintained throughout the 14th century, but it made Italy a temptingly weak target for foreign invaders. In 1494, the French took Florence, Rome, and Naples in quick succession. In 1508, the pope joined France and Germany in making war on

Venice, and then allied with the Spanish and Germans to kick the French out of Italy. From 1522 to 1559, the Hapsburg-Valois War between the German and French monarchies was frequently fought in Italy. The sack of Rome in 1527 by Charles V of France was particularly devastating.

In Sandro Botticelli's *The Birth of Venus* (c. 1485), the gods of the wind and the breeze gently blow Venus to the shore, where she is greeted by the goddess of spring. The flowers in the background represent the rose, which was said to have flowered for the first time at Venus's birth.

goddess's simplified features embody the ideal Classical beauty, but a faraway expression in her eyes hints at an inner world of thoughts and emotions that was missing from Classical art. Although the background is flat, the emphasis on bone structure beneath her flesh is in keeping with Renaissance preoccupations with the depiction of volume and faithful anatomy.

Leonardo used the new techniques of perspective to define space in his *Last Supper* (1498). Unfortunately, he was less successful with his experiments in making new kinds of paint. The *Last Supper* deteriorated quickly, and today it is difficult to appreciate the true value of the painting. Nonetheless, Leonardo's genius manages to shine through the decay. The painting portrays the dramatic moment when Christ announces to his disciples that one of them will betray him. The figures are dynamic and charged with tension and emotion. According to one story, Leonardo was so concerned about getting the expressions and gestures right that the prior, or head, of the monastery in which the work was being painted became impatient. He complained that Leonardo would come in and stare at the painting for hours, make half a dozen brush strokes, and leave. Leonardo replied that he was having trouble depicting the face of the traitor Judas Iscariot, but if the prior was in a hurry, he could just use the prior's face as a model. The results were worth the wait; despite its poor condition, Leonardo's *Last Supper* continues to bring him fame.

Unlike traditional paintings of the Last Supper, Leonardo's work does not depict Judas in front of the table at the center of the painting, but rather as the fourth disciple from the left, reaching for the bread.

Leonardo's most famous work and one of the most celebrated portraits ever painted, the *Mona Lisa* has been greatly admired and much copied since its creation, coming to be seen as the standard for Renaissance portraits.

When the young sculptor Michelangelo created the *David*, he did not portray the hero after he has slain the giant, as had traditionally been done, but rather in the tense moments before the battle.

The sculpture that made Michelangelo famous was the *David*. At 15 feet (4.5 m) tall, it was the largest free-standing statue since the Classical period. Although it depicts the Biblical hero who defeated the giant warrior Goliath, Michelangelo drew upon Classical sculpture to create an image of ideal beauty. The statue's proportions are so perfect that it is still copied and used as a model today. David is depicted naked, and the slingshot in his hand is barely visible; his strength comes from within, from his moral courage and religious faith. The republic of Florence needed a symbol of spiritual strength; after the death of Lorenzo de' Medici in 1492, power struggles and a French invasion had torn the city apart. At Michelangelo's request, the statue was placed before the Palazzo Vecchio, Florence's seat of government. Michelangelo wrote in his diary that it stood there as "a symbol of our Republic" and "a warning" that "whoever governed Florence should govern justly and defend it bravely."

Leonardo's *Mona Lisa* (c. 1505) is believed to have begun as a commissioned portrait of a Florentine government official's wife. But for unknown reasons, the painting was never delivered to the official. Leonardo took it with him whenever he traveled, and it is even said that the *Mona Lisa* stood at his bedside when he lay dying. Its realism is striking; one of Leonardo's contemporaries observed that "on looking at the pit of the throat one could swear that the pulses were beating." The artist's brush strokes can be seen only under a microscope. But realism is not what has made the painting an object of fascination for centuries. Leonardo once said, "A good painter is to paint two things, namely man and the working of man's mind. The first is easy, the second difficult." Mona Lisa's steady gaze, ambiguous half-smile,

Raphael painted this youthful self-portrait at the age of 23, shortly after he had arrived in Florence to study the works being created by great Renaissance masters such as Leonardo and Michelangelo.

and relaxed pose, partly turned away from the viewer, draw one's attention to her state of mind, but it is impossible to say what it might be. The feeling of something unknown but powerful is enhanced by the smoky blending of her hair and clothing with the wild, inhospitable landscape of the background, so that she seems to materialize out of it.

Raphael is known for his ability to unify a variety of figures against a detailed background in one grand, harmonized design. In his design for the *Stanza della Segnatura* (1509–11), the pope's library in the Vatican Palace, the walls are decorated with four large frescoes, each representing an area of human endeavor: *The Disputation Concerning the Blessed Sacrament* represents religion, *The School of Athens* philosophy, *The Cardinal Virtues* justice, and *Parnassus* poetry. Within each fresco, a large room seems to retreat through a series of arches. Classical influences are apparent in both the architecture and the people pictured. Ancient Greek and Roman gods and poets preside from the ceiling, and *The School of Athens* is populated by Classical philosophers such as Aristotle and Plato. Many of the philosophers' faces, however, are those of contemporary artists. Michelangelo reclines on the steps as Heraclitus, Leonardo appears as Plato, and architect Donato Bramante (1444–1514) is Euclid. Raphael himself stands beside Ptolemy in the lower right-hand corner, looking directly out of the painting as if to connect past and present.

In 1506, Raphael's friend Bramante was chosen by the pope to design a new church to replace St. Peter's Basilica, which had been built in the fourth century and was deteriorating. The old church was pulled down so that the new St. Peter's could be built in the same place, which was thought to be the site of St. Peter's grave. Bramante's design drew upon the principles of

Created by several Renaissance masters, St. Peter's Basilica is the world's largest church, with a capacity of more than 60,000. Nearly every square foot is adorned with sculptures, paintings, and tapestries from Italy's greatest artists.

Classical architecture, using pillars and arches to define space and emphasize perspective. When Bramante died in 1514, Raphael took over. Numerous famous artists and architects succeeded him during the more than 120 years required to complete the building. Michelangelo was primarily responsible for the design of the great dome when he held the job from 1546 until his death in 1564. When it was finally finished, St. Peter's dominated Rome's skyline, a symbol of the city's place as the capital of Christianity and a crowning achievement of the Renaissance.

THE END OF THE RENAISSANCE

The height of the Renaissance during the first quarter of the 16th century was centered on Rome. With the death of Raphael in 1520 and the brutal pillaging of Rome by French forces in 1527, the artists who had gathered there began to disperse around Europe. At about the same time, the explorations of Christopher Columbus and others were causing an explosion of new knowledge. The growing storm of the Protestant Reformation had finally broken, causing sweeping transformations in European culture and politics. Although great Renaissance art continued to be created during the late 16th century, the Renaissance style slowly began to be diluted and to grow in different directions.

As the Renaissance style of art began to be replaced with new forms, great changes were also happening elsewhere in the world, as Europeans were exploring new lands such as Hispaniola, shown opposite in a woodcut that was published with a letter from Christopher Columbus detailing his discoveries in the New World.

One new direction was the Mannerist movement, which drew upon the drama, rich color, and technical sophistication of the Renaissance, but abandoned its Classical influences and their emphasis on harmony of organization. In Venice, Tintoretto (Jacopo Robusti, 1518–94), one of Titian's students, was an important early contributor to Mannerism. He claimed to want to combine the color of Titian with the drawing of Michelangelo, but his style was a significant departure from the Renaissance. Tintoretto's *Last Supper* takes the energy and psychological insight of Leonardo's portrayal of the scene to a new extreme; the painting is crowded with figures, and the light and shadows suggest frantic movement. Jesus shines with a supernatural light, and ghostly angels hover above him. The skewed perspective, with the table at a diagonal, is radically different from traditional depictions. Deliberate distortion of space and intense spirituality were hallmarks of Mannerist art.

Another painter in the Mannerist tradition, El Greco ("The Greek," Domenicos Theoteokopoulos, 1541–1614), traveled to Venice from his native Greece to study art. About 10 years later he went to Spain, where he remained for the rest of his life. His paintings have the luminosity and rich color of the Venetian Renaissance, but his crowded style and intense emotionalism are Mannerist. In stark contrast to Renaissance style, his paintings lack any depiction of space or perspective. In *The Burial of Count Orgaz* (1586), for example, the arrangement of the figures, lined up at the same close distance, is very flat. The painting is crowded with people; even the space directly above their heads is filled with angels and saints looking down from heaven.

During the late 16th and early 17th centuries, the Mannerist style would evolve into the theatrical movement and drama of the Baroque period. But

A NEW WORLD

In 1492, Italian explorer Christopher Columbus set out from Spain to find a sea route to Asia. He landed on the Caribbean island of Hispaniola, occupied today by Haiti and the Dominican Republic. Although he called it a "New World," Columbus did not yet realize what he had found. In 1519, Ferdinand Magellan of Portugal set out to try again for a direct route to Asia. He sailed

to present-day Brazil and continued south around the tip of South America, landing on the islands known today as the Philippines. Magellan died there, but his crew completed the trip around the southern tip of Africa to Spain—confirming that the Earth is round, and much larger than anyone had thought.

Although El Greco moved away from Renaissance styles and painted in the Mannerist tradition—as in his *Sacred Family* (c. 1580–85), which demonstrates the elongated figures and lack of empty space characteristic of this movement—his works still demonstrate the influence of Renaissance painters such as Michelangelo.

Baroque art moved away from the distortions of Mannerism. Artists returned to the careful, naturalistic representation of the observed world emphasized during the Renaissance, building upon it to reach new levels of technical proficiency. The Baroque movement also revived Classical influences; artists incorporated mythological references, created balanced and harmonious compositions, and idealized depictions of people and landscapes.

The explosion of Protestantism was a major factor in the changing face of art during the 16th century. A German friar named Martin Luther and other leaders of the Protestant Reformation denounced the ornate religious art that decorated Catholic churches as sacrilegious idol worship. After 1530, there were no more altarpieces painted in Germany. Artists in Protestant countries, such as Germany and Switzerland, had to adapt the thematic concerns of their art or else leave to seek new patrons in Catholic countries, such as Italy and France. On the other hand, the Protestant emphasis on personal worship of God meant that small Bible scenes suitable for hanging in people's homes became very popular.

For Catholic artists, there were new instructions announced by the Catholic Church in 1545. In an effort to prevent conversions to Protestantism, art was to be used as a vehicle to appeal to middle and lower class people, especially those who were illiterate. In particular, the lives of popular saints and instructive depictions of Christian virtues were to be presented in ways that could be easily understood. The Church's instructions were one source of the intense emotionalism and accessible realism of the emerging Baroque movement. These themes had begun to emerge during the Renaissance, and they reached their height in Baroque art.

THE PROTESTANT REFORMATION

By the end of the Middle Ages, the pope had become immersed in politics and amassed a great deal of power and wealth. This preoccupation with worldly affairs, as well as the accompanying corruption, undermined the Catholic Church's spiritual authority, and there were increasing calls for reform. In 1517, a German friar named Martin Luther posted his "Ninety-Five Theses" on the door of a church in Germany. He emphasized personal faith and declared that the Bible was the only authority. In 1536, John Calvin, a French lawyer who fled to Switzerland after converting to the Protestant cause, published the first comprehensive treatise of the movement. By the middle of the 16th century, Protestantism dominated northern Europe and had begun to spread.

Filippo Brunelleschi, who helped to create the Renaissance style, became a famous architect and was hailed as a Florentine hero because of his magnificent design for the dome on the city's cathedral.

The Renaissance had a profound impact on art and the world beyond the Baroque period, even up to today. Before the Renaissance, European art was used for religious instruction and illustration, or for the decoration of buildings and objects. The Renaissance saw an increase in secular subjects, beginning with Classical mythology and portraits and extending to scenes from everyday life and landscapes. Eventually, this trend would lead in the 19th and 20th centuries to the idea of "art for the sake of art." It also marked a more generalized move toward secularism, as European culture increasingly emphasized the power of individuals to shape their world.

Another important change during the Renaissance was a new respect for art and artists. This involved not only an improved position in society for artists, but a new phenomenon: the celebrity artist. Pioneering biographies of artists were published during the Renaissance. Increasingly, there was a

Titian, who painted *Venus of Urbino* (1538) for an Italian prince, was a famed artist throughout Europe by the 1530s. With works ranging from pagan pageantry to religious tragedy, Titian's revolutionary artistic techniques inspired future generations of artists.

fascination with the life and personality of the artist. Romanticized accounts often depicted such artists as Leonardo and Michelangelo as solitary, conflicted creative geniuses. This conception of the artist would reach its height in the 19th century, but it began during the Renaissance.

The new respect for art meant that it was seen as an intellectual and creative process, rather than a matter of sheer physical skill. Artists began writing books about art theory and method. Dürer, for example, wrote treatises on measurement, proportion, anatomy, and perspective, and a handbook for young artists. Artists began to study mathematical and scientific subjects and their application to art, and to participate in intellectual discussions with scholars and other artists. Some of these discussions led to a slow awakening to the problematic split between creating faithful representations of the observed world and expressing a perspective or inner mental state. The understanding of art commonly held today is based on these fundamental shifts. The great Renaissance paintings, frescoes, sculptures, and buildings that have drawn crowds for more than 400 years laid the foundation for modern art.

Reflecting the new focus on intellectualism in art during the Renaissance, Leonardo's famous drawing *Vitruvian Man* (1492, opposite) is a detailed study of human proportions. Michelangelo, too, focused on the realistic depiction of the human form, as can be seen in his *Creation of Adam* (1510, above) from the Sistine Chapel ceiling.

TIMELINE

1414	The first of a series of councils held by the Catholic Church meets in Germany
1424	Masolino and Masaccio begin the Brancacci Chapel frescoes
1432	Jan van Eyck completes the *Ghent Altarpiece*
1434	Jan van Eyck paints *The Arnolfini Marriage*
	The Medici family takes control of Florence
1446	Fra Angelico's *Annunciation* is complete
1452	Johann Gutenberg invents a method of printing books in Germany
1453	Constantinople, capital of the Byzantine empire, falls to the Ottoman Turks
1479	A unified Spain is created by the marriage of Isabella of Castile and Ferdinand II of Aragon
1484	Botticelli paints *The Birth of Venus*
1492	Christopher Columbus lands in the New World
	Lorenzo de' Medici dies, beginning a power struggle in Florence
1498	Leonardo paints his *Last Supper*
1504	Michelangelo completes *David*
1505	Leonardo paints the *Mona Lisa*
1506	Work begins on the new St. Peter's Basilica
1511	Raphael completes his frescoes in the *Stanza della Segnatura*
1512	Michelangelo completes the ceiling of the Sistine Chapel
1513	Dürer completes *The Passion*, a series of wood engravings
1517	Martin Luther calls for Reformation of the Catholic Church
1527	Rome is invaded by French forces
1541	Michelangelo completes *The Last Judgment*
1550	Giorgio Vasari's book *Lives of the Most Excellent Painters, Sculptors, and Architects* is published
1559	Titian completes *Diana and Callisto*
1564	The dome of St. Peter's Basilica is completed

GLOSSARY

altarpiece   an ornamental painting or carving placed above and behind an altar

anatomy   the structure of a living thing, especially the human body

apprentice   a person who works for a craftsman or other skilled person in exchange for instruction in the craft or skill

Classical   relating to Roman and Greek culture from about 500 B.C. to about A.D. 500

commissions   requests for works of art to be made to order, in exchange for money

craftsmen   workers in skilled trades, such as weavers and carpenters

Eucharist   bread and wine that has been blessed and that symbolizes the sacrifice made by Jesus Christ

frescoes   paintings made on wet plaster with watercolors, so that when the plaster dries the paint crystallizes on the wall

guilds   independent associations of bankers, professionals, or craftsmen

harmonious   having parts combined in an orderly and pleasing arrangement

meditation   deep reflection on sacred matters as an act of worship

Middle Ages   the period of European history from the end of the Roman Empire in A.D. 476 to about 1450; also called the medieval period

patron   during the Renaissance, a wealthy person who supported an artist financially and gave him or her commissions

perspective   the changed appearance of objects according to their distance and position

philosophical   relating to the study of human conduct, thought, knowledge, and the nature of the universe

pope   the bishop of Rome and head of the Catholic Church

portraits   paintings or drawings of a single person

relief   sculpture that projects slightly from a flat surface

secular   relating to worldly things, as opposed to religious matters

themes   subjects or ideas that dominate and unify a work of art

wood engravings   pictures made by cutting into a block of wood, leaving raised lines which are coated with ink and pressed onto paper

INDEX